Josef Originals

Charming Figurines with Price Guide

Dee Harris

Jim & Kaye Whitaker

Schiffer Publishing Ltd

77 Lower Valley Road, Atglen, PA 19310

Dedication

This book is dedicated to the memory of Muriel Joseph George.

Acknowledgments

A book like this would not be possible without the help of avid collectors. We would like to thank the many people who opened their homes and their collections for us to photograph. Special thanks to collectors Gloria Fogel, Rita Miller, Betty Nelson, Jenni Perkinson and Ellen Wooster. We would also like to extend our thanks to dealers Shirley Rogers of Lafayette Schoolhouse, Lafayette, Oregon, and Ralph Hickman of Inland Empire Showcase, Pomona, California.

Since the beginning of this project we have heard from many people who have offered information and/or photos. For their help, we wish to express our appreciation to Judy Barrick, Judy Farone, Robert Foldes, Sharon Krohn, Barbara Maxon, Linda Nothnagel, Mary Ann Royce, Margery Singleton, Terry and Arlene Tersey, Karen Wagner and Will and Karen Winn.

Deepest appreciation to Muriel's granddaughter Victoria Stocker for her time and assistance. Thanks, too, to George Good, Muriel's partner, for his input into the history.

The photography was made possible by the equipment loaned to us by Mark Mooney and James E. Whitaker, Sr.—we are very appreciative.

Photography and Cover Photography by Jim Whitaker

Copyright © 1994 by Dolores Harris, Jim & Kaye Whitaker
Library of Congress Catalog Number: 94-65614

Printed in Hong Kong
ISBN: 0-88740-647-5

We are interested in hearing from authors with book ideas on related topics.

Designed by Mark S. Balbach

Published by Schiffer Publishing Ltd.
77 Lower Valley Road
Atglen, PA 19310
Please write for a free catalog.
This book may be purchased from the publisher.
Please include $2.95 postage.
Try your bookstore first.

Contents

The Story of Muriel Joseph George, Creator of the Figurines

The wonderful figures in this book all began in the talented hands of Muriel Joseph George. Yes, the spelling is actually *Joseph,* but the printer made an error when printing the first labels for the sale of Pitty Sing, and time did not permit them to correct it—so the name became "Josef Originals."

In 1942, Muriel made lucite jewelry under the name "Muriel of California." But during World War II, when she could no longer get lucite, she turned to clay modeling and produced ceramic jewelry. Clay was plentiful, even in wartime, and the feel of it in her hands must have been comforting. Years later she said she had "just always" modeled. Muriel made girls, pixie children, animals and set them to dry or destroyed them. Sometimes her work was serious, sometimes it was whimsical.

Then, at last, the war was over and Tom George, her soon-to-be husband, was coming home. He was not able to work for a year. She continued to model—Chinese children in big coolie hats, a graceful Chinese couple, mice, puppies, kittens, but never a Japanese figure. Pearl Harbor was too fresh in memories. Muriel modeled what she admired, liked and understood. For Tom it was a time of frustration, moving from war activity to a semi-invalid condition. He eased the problem by making molds from her clay models. It was 1946 and they talked about opening their own pottery company.

In that heady post-war climate, a dream had an excellent chance of coming to fruition. Muriel and Tom worked out of their garage until they could afford to rent a building. The first commercial figure, Pitty Sing, was done in the garage. He was a small Chinese boy in a big coolie hat, sitting, asleep, with a cat on his lap. Muriel's father took this figure to a Broadway department store. They gave him an order for two gross, and she went to work. The hat gave them trouble in the kiln; it would break or slip. Muriel was ever after hesitant about putting hats on her figurines. We know she did it, but as she said, "never on a birthday girl." Their logo was molded on the circular base, an incised script "Josef Originals" and the encircled "C". Other figures began to sell. They were surprised at the volume.

Always a perfectionist, Muriel kept the hairstyles up to date, from short to bouffant to curly. She made different sets: the "Morning, Noon and Night" set, the "Four Seasons" set, and the "Days of the Week" set, to name a few. Since the orders came in dozens, she made figurines in singles, pairs, and sets of three, four, six,

and twelve. She used her employees as inspiration for models. She soon had between ten and twelve employees, and plenty of models.

Muriel never made figurines for Disney (that prize went to Vernon Kilns, Hagen-Renaker and others) but she did design a belt for Disney made of a series of circles. Because she never made Disney figures, her creations remained the work of her own genius, never copies of some other person's inspiration.

During the 1950s, Muriel and Tom became aware that copies were appearing on the market. The copies were inferior and poorly-painted, and they might be changed in small ways—a hat or a flower might be different—but they could bear the incised logo. They were coming from Japan! The market was flooded with cheap copies of Muriel's work. This not only stole her sales, but her reputation as well.

In response, Muriel produced new models of unmistakable excellence. Hedy and Teddy are some of the new figures made in 1953. Since they had to charge more for these "made in California" figurines, however, they continued to lose sales to the inexpensive Japanese imitations.

Around 1954 Muriel and Tom met George Good, a representative and distributor for many of the Calforina pottery lines, including Hagen-Renaker and Rose Lane. In 1959 sales had dropped about seventy-five percent, so George persuaded Muriel and Tom to form a partnership, "George Imports," and to go to Japan where labor was cheap to have their figurines produced. On January 1, 1974 the company merged with other George Good lines and became the "George-Good Corporation"—George for Muriel Joseph George, and Good for George Good.

In late 1959, Muriel, Tom and George went to Japan to the Katayama Factory owned by the Katayama family. They produced some of the finest work being done in Japan at that time. Muriel spent six weeks in Japan, working with the people at the factory to teach them her ways. Telling about it thirty years later, she said, "six weeks and I made life-long friends." When she came home she created new designs, and sent colored drawings and instructions to the factory in Japan to be produced. With her approval, in due time, the finished product was shipped to her, and her prices were once more competitive.

Business boomed again. Muriel's creativity boomed also. She created elegant Victorian ladies, music boxes, "Little Internationals," "Birthstone Dolls," and "Birthday Girls." Muriel also made elephants, ostriches, frogs, owls, cats, dogs, monkeys and the famous mice.

Muriel made dozens of mice. More than forty different ones have been documented. One of her large orders was from a cheese manufacturer who ordered $40,000 worth of mice to give away with a cheese promotion.

The logo remained the same—the incised "Josef Originals" and the "C" in a circle, molded into the unglazed base of the girls. Few animals, however, were large enough for the incised mark. Instead they carry a round or oval sticker, black with gold lettering and border, and a quarter inch oval sticker which says "Japan".

Muriel Joseph George retired in 1980-81, and George Good bought the company from her. She continued to design for him until 1984-85. Muriel did all the design work, with her daughter, Diane, coming in to help from 1973 to 1986. George Good sold the company to Applause, Inc. in 1985, and no new designs can be made under the Josef Originals name.

Though Muriel Joseph George died in 1992, her legacy remains in the work of her talented hands—in hundreds of bright children, beautiful people and charming animals. We haven't yet found all of them, but the hunt is on!

"Pitty Sing" with a brown hat, 4"

"Pitty Sing" with a red hat

"Pitty Sing" with a green hat

"Yong Chee"

"Wee Ching"

Chinese girl with a kitten

"Wee Ching" with a dog, and girl with a kitten

Chinese boy with a blue hat

Chinese boy with a black hat

Chinese boy, 2 1/2" tall

Chinese boy head/
shoulder figure

Chinese boy and girl with a goose

"Wu Fu," 10" tall

"Wu Cha," 10" tall

8

"Cho Cho," 10 3/4" tall

"Sakura," 10 3/4" tall

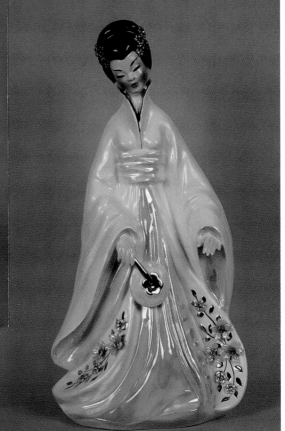

"Japan," 10 1/4 tall

Chinese girl with her fan down, and "Autumn Leaf" with her fan up, 4 1/2"

"Little TV," 5 1/4"

Girl sitting in a white dress, planter, 4 3/4"

"Penny," in a light green dress, 4"

"Penny," in a rose dress, 4"

"Penny," in a white dress, 4"

"The Prince," 3 3/4"

"April" and "Carol," 4 1/4"

"Teddy" and "Hedy," 4 1/4"

"Holiday" and "Sunny," 4 1/4

"Bongo" and "Congo," 4 1/4"

"Poi and Koi"

Mother holding a baby

"Mama" in a violet dress, with a book, 7 1/4"

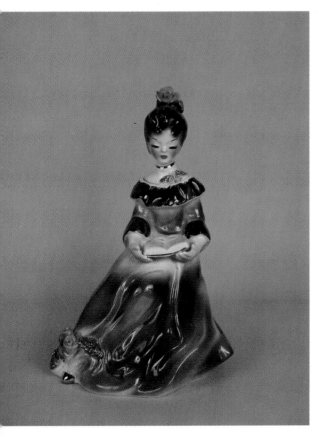

"Mama" in a blue dress, with a book, 7 1/4"

"Mary Ann"

"Mary Ann"

"Mama" in a rose dress, 7 1/4"

"Mama" in a blue dress, 7 1/4"

"Mary Ann"

"Mary Ann"

"Mama," 7 1/4"

"Mama" in a lime green dress

"Mary Ann" and "Mama"

"Mary Ann"

"Mary Ann"

"Mary Ann," and "Mama" in a rose dress

4" half dolls

4" half doll

4" half doll

"Sylvia," 5 3/4"

"Molly" in a yellow dress, planter, 5"

"Molly" in a light brown dress, planter, 5"

"Victoria," 6"

"Victoria," 6"

"Cleo"

"Cleo" and "Gail"

"Gail"

"Charmaine"

"Cleo"

Girl with parasol

"Gabrielle" and "Jacques," 5 1/2"

Girl in blue dress with rose, 5 1/2"

"Juliette," 5 1/2"

Girl in rose dress

"Charmaine," 5 1/2"

"Melissa"

"Claudia," 5 3/4"

"Missy"

"Amy," 5 1/2"

"Joseph II"

"Kandy" and "Taffy"

"Kandy"

"Carol"

"Holly"

"Mickey" and "Melinda," 3 1/4"

"Melinda"

"Cindy"

"Denise," 5 1/2"

Girl with a kitten

"Party Dress"

"Little Gift"

"Tea Time"

Girl sitting with a basket

"Lullaby" and "Good Night"

Girl in a light blue dress

"Secret Pal," in a rose dress and in a green dress

"Little Tutu"

"Now I lay me," "Down to sleep"

"Good Luck" Angel

Tuesday, from the "Days of the Week" series

Monday, from the "Days of the Week" series

Wednesday, from the "Days of the Week" series

Thursday, from the "Days of the Week" series

Friday, from the "Days of the Week" series

Saturday, from the "Days of the Week" series

Sunday, from the "Days of the Week" series

27

January

February

December

March

May

November

October

September

June

July

August

"Dinner Belle" and "Chapel Belle"

"Southern Belle" and "Vesper Belle"

"Ding Dong Belle"

"Christmas Belle"

"Mission Belle"

"Wedding Belle"

From the "Belle" series

From the "Belle" series

From the "Belle" series

January, from the "Dolls of the Month" series,
3 1/4"

April, from the "Dolls of the Month" series, 3 1/4"

February, from the "Dolls of the Month" series,
3 1/4"

May, from the "Dolls of the Month" series, 3 1/4"

March, from the "Dolls of the Month" series, 3 1/4"

July, from the "Dolls of the Month" series, 3 1/4"

August, from the "Dolls of the Month" series,
3 1/4"

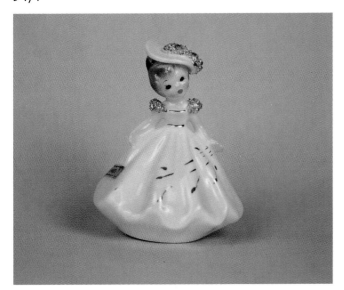

September, from the "Dolls of the Month" series,
3 1/4"

October, from the "Dolls of the Month" series,
3 1/4"

November, from the "Dolls of the Month" series,
3 1/4"

December, from the "Dolls of the Month" series, 3 1/4"

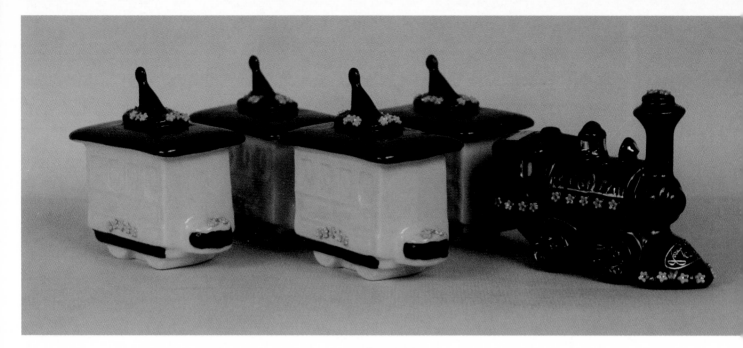

"Atlas" C1954

"Wee Three"

Kitten

34

Chapter Two:
The Prolific Years
1959-1985, Working in Japan

The following twenty-nine figures are from the "Little Internationals" series. The original set included figures representing eighteen countries, and more were added through the years. Each figurine is 3 1/2" tall.

"America"

"Africa"

"Austria"

"China"

"England"

"France"

"Germany"   "Greece"   "Hawaii"

"Hawaii"   "Hungary"   "Holland"

"India"

"Ireland"

"Ireland"

"Ireland"

"Israel"

"Mexico"

"Japan"

"Italy"

"Mexico"

"Poland"

"Norway"

"Portugal"

"Russia"

"Scotland"

"Wee Japanese Kabuki" playing Japanese instruments:
Shakuhachi, Ougi, and Tsuzumi

"Spain"

"Sweden"

"Wee Japanese Kabuki" playing Japanese instruments:
Shamisen, Kodaiko, and Tategoto

"Switzerland"

"Housekeepers," marked on the box "Frying Egg," "Ironing," and "Cookie Tray"

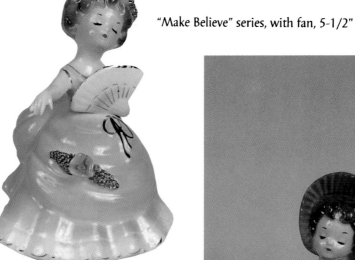

"Make Believe" series, with fan, 5-1/2"

"Make Believe" series, with tea set, 5-1/2"

"Housekeepers," marked on the box "Tea Pot," "Drying Dishes," and "On Phone"

"Make Believe" series, with hand mirror, 5-1/2"

Not pictured in the "Make Believe" series are figures with rhinestone shoes, with pearls, and with a parasol.

"Birthday Party Girls" series, with
birthday cake, 5-1/4"

"The Little Pets" series, with butterfly, 5 1/4"

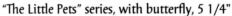

"The Little Pets" series,
with bird, 5-1/4"

Not pictured with in the "Birthday Party Girls" series are
figurines with ice cream, with a teacup, with a piece of cake,
with candles, and with a gift package.

"The Little Pets" series, with a
Pekingese, 5-1/4"

"Chinese Girl" series, six in set, with
story tags, 5" high.

"Moon Beam" from "The Flower
Sprites" series, six in set, 3 3/ 4"

Not pictured in "The Little Pets" series are figurines
holding a rabbit, with a spaniel, and holding a kitten.

Not pictured from "The Flower Sprites" series are "Rain
Drop," "Little Flower," "Butterfly," "Sun Beam," and "Spring
Song."

"For Baby" and "Bon Voyage" from the "Greetings" series, six
in set 4"

Not pictured from "The Greetings" set are "Thank You,"
"Secret Pal," "Happy Birthday," and "Get Well."

"Birthday Girls"

"Birthday Girls"

"Birthday Girls"

"Birthday Girls"

"Birthday Girl"

"Birthday Girl"

"Birthday Girl"

"Birthday Girl"

"Birthday Girl"

"Birthday Girl"

"Birthday Girl"

"Birthstone Dolls" for January, February, and March, 3 1/2"

"Birthstone Dolls" for April, May, and June

"Birthstone Dolls" for July, August, and September

"Birthstone Dolls" for October, November, and December

Soap dish

Girl pin box

Lipstick holder

Lipstick holders

Nun rosary holder

Planter series

Doll with the caption "Pray Daily"

"Doll of the Month," January, 3 1/2"

"Doll of the Month," April

"Doll of the Month," February

"Doll of the Month," May

"Doll of the Month," March

"Doll of the Month," June

"Doll of the Month," July

"Doll of the Month," October

"Doll of the Month," August

"Doll of the Month," November

"Doll of the Month," September

"Doll of the Month," December

"Dinner Belle"

Christmas Bell

"Belle of the Ball"

"Church Belle"

50

From the "Belle" series

"Southern Belle"

"Wedding Belle"

"School Belle"

Babies with kittens

Ballerinas

Little girls

Ballerinas

Baby with a kitten on a pillow

"Pennies from Heaven"

"First Communion"

"Peaches & Cream"

"Party Line"

"Hearts & Flowers"

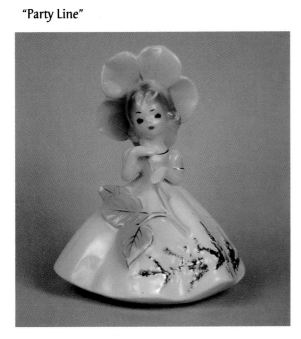

"Miss America"

"Mighty Like a Rose"

"Pisces"

"Pretty as a Picture"

"Puppy Love"

"Sitting Pretty"

"Gemini"

"Shy as a Violet"

"The Bridal Party" bride and groom, 4"

"The Little Guest"

Girl with a rose basket

"The Bridal Party" bridesmaid, 4"

Not pictured from "The Bridal Party" series is the bridesmaid in pink.

"The New Baby" from the "Special Occasions" series

"Happy Anniversary" from the "Special Occasions" series

Graduation Angel in a blue gown

"Graduate" from the "Special Occasions" series, Boy Graduation Angel

Graduation Angel in a Pink Gown

"Jill" from the "Nursery Rhymes" series, 4" high

"An Arm Full of Love" series, figure with a puppy

"An Arm Full of Love" series, figure with a present

"An Arm Full of Love" series, figure with roses

Girl with a poodle

From the "Party Cake Toppers" series, a boy and girl dancing, 3"

Not pictured from "An Arm Full of Love" series are figures with kittens, with birds, and with a baby.

Girl with a cake

"Baby Shower" from the "Party
Cake Toppers" series, 4" high

"I Love You"

Girls with cake and with fruit

"Bride" and girl with a bird

Girl with flowers

Girl with a water pot

Girl with a tea cup

Girl with a kitten

Girl with a serving tray

Girl with a mirror

"Bridal Shower" from the "Special Occasion" series, 4 1/2" high

Girl from the "Make Believe" series, 4 1/2" high

"Shower" from the "Party Cake Toppers" series, 4" high

"Sugar & Spice"

"Debby" from the "First Love" series, 5" high

Girl with a puppy

"Flower Girl" from the "Bridal Group" series, 4 1/4" high

Girl with a present, in a rose dress

Boy with flowers

Girl with a present, in a light blue dress

"Violets" from the "Flower Girl" series, 5 1/2" high

"Birthday" candle holder from the "Party Cake Toppers" series, 4" high

Girl from "Morning, Noon, and Night" series, 5 3/4" high

Girl from "First Formal" series, 5 1/4" high

Girl from "Morning, Noon, and Night" series, 5 3/4" high

"Roses" from the "Flower Girl" series, 5 1/2" high

Girl from "Morning, Noon, and Night" series, 5 3/4" high

Girl from "Morning, Noon, and Night" series, 5 3/4" high

Girl with a book

"Holiday in Hawaii" from the "Holiday Girls" series, 5 1/2" high

"Susan" from the "First Formal" series,
5 1/4" high

"Holiday in England" from the "Holiday Girls"
series, 5 1/2" high

Girl from ""First Formal" series, 5 1/4" high

"Lipstick" from the " First Time" series, 4 1/2" high

"Summer" from the "Four Seasons" series, 5 3/4" high

"Mary Lou" from the "First Formal" series, 5 1/4" high

Girl from the "First Formal" series, 5 1/4" high

"Meg" from the "First Formal" series, 5 1/4" high

"Pansies" from the "Flower Girl" series, 5 1/2" high

Girl from the "Joy of Spring" series

Girl from the "Joy of Spring" series

Girl with a bird on her shoulder

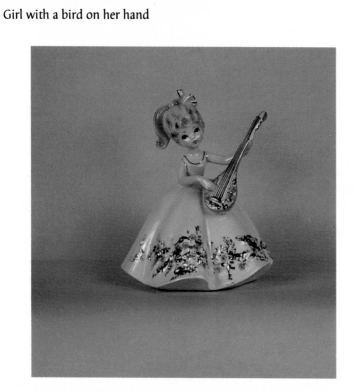

Girl with a bird on her hand

Girl from the "Joy of Spring" series

"Bonnie" from the "Musicale" series, 6"

"Robin" from the "Musicale" series, 6"

66

"Mandy" from the "Musicale" series, 6"

"Bess" from the "Musicale" series, 6"

"Penny" from the "Musicale" series, 6" high

"Tammy" from the "Musicale" series, 6" high

"Love Story" from the "Romance" series, 8" high

"The Courtship" from the "Romance" series, 8" high

"The Engagement," with a large diamond ring, from the "Romance" series, 8" high

Girl with a ring box

"The Trousseau," a girl wearing a diamond ring, from the "Romance" series, 8" high

Baby shower gift

"Tea for Two," girl wearing wedding band, 8"

"Dinner for Two," a girl wearing a wedding band, 8"

"Louise" from the Colonial Days series, 9 1/2" high

Colonial Days series, 9 1/2" high

Colonial Days series, 9 1/2" high

"Caroline" from the Colonial Days series, 9 1/2" high

Not Pictured from the "Colonial Days" series are figures
in a yellow gown with green ribbons in hat, and in a green
gown with an instrument.

Lady sitting with a dog

Lady standing in a blue gown

Lady with parasol, 8" high.

Lady with a mirror, in a green dress

Lady at a writing desk

Lady with a mirror, in a yellow and
green dress, with a matte finish

Colonial couple, 9" high

Lady with a parasol, in a yellow dress, with a matte finish

"Marie" from the "XVII Century French" series, 7" high

Colonial lady in blue gown with a matte finish

"Love Rendezvous" from "Love Makes the World Go Round" series, 9" high

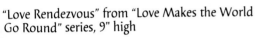

Lady from the "Love Makes the World Go Round" series, 9" high

"Garden Tryst" from the "Love Makes the World Go Round" series, 9" high

"Love Makes The World Go Round" series, 9" high

"Blue Bird" from the "Love Makes The World Go Round" series, 9" high

Not pictured from the "Love Makes the World Go Round" series is "The Love Locket," a figure in a pale yellow gown holding a locket, 9" high.

Not pictured are "Spring" and "Fall."

"Summer," from the "Four Seasons" series

"Winter," from the "Four Seasons" series

"Rose Garden" series, 5" high

"Rose Garden" series, 5" high

Not pictured from the "Rose Garden" series are a yellow figure with a basket, a pink figure with a puppy, a white figure with a bouquet, and a peach figure with a watering can.

Gibson Girls series, set of six, 6 1/2" high

Gibson Girls series, set of six, 6 1/2" high

The "Prom" series, from a set of six

Not pictured from the Gibson Girls series are the following: a standing figure in a pink gown with a hat, using her parasol as a cane; a standing figure in a white gown, holding a flower; a sitting figure in a yellow gown, with a straw hat in her hand; and a figure in a rose gown, leaning on a pillar with her parasol up.

"Parasol Girls" series, one of three known

Not pictured from the "Parasol Girls" series is a sitting figure in a green gown, and a figure in a gold gown with white trim.

"Portraits" series of six, "Ladies of Song" 4 3/4"

"Portraits" series, "Ladies of Song" 4-3/4"

"Portraits" series, "Ladies of Song" 4-3/4"

"Portraits" series, "Ladies of Song" 4-3/4"

Not pictured in this series are figures in a pink gown with
yellow flowers and a parasol, and another in a yellow gown,
standing with a brown hat and a basket.

The "Magnolia" series consists of six "beautiful ladies from the magnificent land of the fragrant Southern Magnolias," each 6 1/2" high.

From the "Magnolia" series

From the "Magnolia" series

From the "Magnolia" series

Not pictured from the "Magnolia" series are the following: a figure in a pale green gown with pink roses on the skirt and a matching parasol; a figure in a pink gown trimmed in rose, with a white fan; and a figure in a yellow gown and matching hat, with a white handkerchief.

The "Gigi" series was a set of six figures, each 7" high. The figures also came as music boxes.

From the "Gigi" series

From the "Gigi" series

From the "Gigi" series

From the "Gigi" series

From the "Gigi" series

Not pictured from the Gigi series is a figure in a peach, ballerina-length dress, black shoes, and a straw hat.

"Bride," 9" high

Lady holding roses, wearing a blue dress

Lady with a bird on her light green dress

Lady in a light green dress

Lady in a peach dress, with a bird

Lady with a flower basket

"The Nurse"

Man with a flower basket

Lady with a butterfly

Girl with a prayer book

Girl with a letter fom the "Victorian Girls Planter" series, 6"
high

Girl from the "Sweet Sixteen" series, 7 1/2" high

Lady reading a book

Girl from the "Summer Days" series

Girl with a rose

Girl with a daisy from the "Sweet Sixteen" series, 7 1/2" high

"Walking in Her Rose Garden" from "A Mother's World" series, 7 1/2" high

"New Hat" from the "Sweet Sixteen" series, 7 1/2" high

"Lady with a Blue Bird"

"Party Dress" from the "Sweet Sixteen" series, 7 1/2" high

Girl from the "Sweet Sixteen" series, 7 1/2" high

Girl holding a bouquet of yellow flowers

Lady in a lavender dress, 8" high, planter

"Buying a New Hat" from "A Mother's World"
series, 7 1/2" high

Lady in a winter coat

"Bride" from the "Romance" series, 7 1/2" high

Catching a bridal bouquet

"Laurel"

"Bride"

Lady in a peach dress

Girl with a puppy

Girl with a parasol

Girl holding a flower

"Say Your Prayers" from the "Little Commandments" series, 3 3/4" high

An angel with a paddle and ball

Cookie angel from the "Little Commandments" series, 3 3/4" high

An angel holding a baby

"Sweet Sister" and "For Baby"

"Happy Birthday"

"Happy Birthday"

"Lara's Theme"

Holding a heart

Holding a present

"Little Green Apples"

"Anniversary Waltz"

"The Bridal March"

"Impossible Dream"

"The Shadow of Your Smile"

Boy and girl with a fan

"You Light Up My Life"

"Fascination"

"Humoresque"

"Love Story"

"A Pretty Girl is Like a Melody"

"Anniversary Waltz"

"Happy Birthday"

Girl in a peach dress

Girl in a green dress

Girl in a yellow dress

"Come to the Cabaret"

"Days of Wine & Roses"

"Skip to My Lou"

"Twinkle, Twinkle Little Star from the "Nursery Rhyme Music Box" series

"My Darling Clementine" from the "Nursery Rhyme Music Box" series

"The Farmer in the Dell" from the "Nursery Rhyme Music Box series

Christmas girl holding a lantern

Girl sewing a flag

Santa Claus

92

Girl listening to a gramaphone

"Romance Music Box" series

"Swan Lake"

"Bridal March"

"Amazing Grace"

"Bridal March"

"Schubert's Lullaby" motherhood music box

Valentine jewel box

"I Love You Truly" golden anniversary music box

Girl with a red, white and blue hat

Girl with a basket, in a white dress with pink trim

Girl with a present, in a white dress with blue trim

Girl with a cake, in a white dress with rose trim

Girl with a present, in a red dress

Girl with a basket, in a red dress

Girl with a cake, in a red dress

Angels with a wreath, and with a basket

Angels with a mandolin, and with a stocking

An angel with a cake

An angel with a music box

Girl with a present

Girl with a present

Girl with a muff

Girl with poinsettias

A set of six Tom and Jerry mugs

Puppies

Kids with a present and a tree

Snowman

Mary, Jesus and Shepherd

Reindeer candle-holders

Deer

"Wee Folks"

"Wee Folks"

"Wee Folks"

"Wee Folks"

An elf with a butterfly

Pixie

Monks

From the "Zodiac" series

Girl with a locket

Girl with a book

Girl with a yellow flower

Girl with a bunny

Girl with a butterfly

Girl with a blue flower

Girl with sunflowers

Girl with a turtle

Girl holding a leaf

"January"

Girl with a dog

Girl from the "Big Sisters and Little Sisters" series

"Colonial Days" series

103

Girl with a doll, from the "Big Sisters and Little Sisters" series

Girl teaching a puppy

Girl with a little boy from the "Big Sisters and Little Sisters" series

Boy with a puppy

Boy eating ice cream

Boy in bed with a puppy

Boy in tent with a puppy

Girl with a ladybug on her dress

"Bride"

Girl with a puppy from the "Little Pets" series

Girl with flowers

Girls with a water pot and a doll

Girl with a pumpkin and a kitten

Girl with kittens

Girl knitting with a kitten

Chapter Three:
Her Animals, A Special Look

Camels, 2-1/2" and 6-3/4"

Ostrich family: mama & papa, each 5" tall, and babies, each 1/2"

Hippo family, 2 1/2", 1", and 2 1/2"   Hippo

Kangaroos, 1-1/2" and 6"

Elephant family, 4-1/2", 2-1/2", and 4-1/2"   Bull, 2-3/4"

Elephant children

Elephant with a swatter

Elephant kids

Mother with a baby

Bears, 2-1/2", 3-3/4", and 1-3/4"

"Bed Bug"

Penguin, 4-3/4"

Horse

Knitting mouse & "Postee"
(Mice range from 1/2" to 2")

A mouse eating, and another entitled "Troubles"

"Soapy" and "Bride"

Mice: one blowing a bubble, another with a valentine, and a third with a teddy mouse

"Old Grand Dad" with children

"Milky Way," babies in a nutshell, and "Talkee"

Mice: with cheese, and looking at a lady bug

Mice: with cake, and writing "I love you"

Four mice: one named "Peanuts," one with a flower hat, one with bubble gum, and one with cheese

Mice

Mice: "Proud Papa," with cheese, with rattle, and a nurse mouse

"Graduate" with bow on tail, and with candle

Mouse planter

Mice: singing carols, with a white tummy, and with a Christmas stocking

Three Christmas mice

Mice: with a candy cane, and with a present

Mice: singing, and writing

Three Christmas mice

Mother with litter, 1/2" to 1" high

Mom with three kittens, playing with a ball, a bird, and a slipper

Mom with three kittens, 2"

Kittens playing with yarn

Cat looking into fish bowl

Three Christmas kittens

Mom with kitten

Boy and girl Siamese cats

Dad and Mom with kitten tabby; all three are type cats

Two cats

Dad and Mom with kids

"Honey," "Tiger," "Sweetheart," and "Amber;" two names
unknown

Three kittens with bibs and bows

Three kittens

Three kittens playing with a turtle

Five kittens

Two tabby cats

Three music boxes

Pair of puppies

Kitten music box; the small kitten dances

Four puppies

Two boxer dogs

Fox

Chihuahua

German shepherd

Monkeys

Monkeys: one holding its tail, another playing cards, and a third looking in a mirror

Squirrels, a ladybug, a puppy, and a monkey

Bees

Caterpillars

Turtle and ladybug

Frogs: with a bee, with a turtle, and with a ladybug

Frog, rooster, and turtle

Frog with a ladybug, sleeping

Two frogs

Rabbits: with a frog,, and with a lollipop

Two rabbits

Skunk

Bunny

Mama rabbit, and a baby with peanut butter

Rabbits

Baby ducks with a caterpillar

Pig family

Pigs

Duck family

Mama duck and baby

Squirrels on a music box

Owls

Pig

Pie bird

Chapter Four:
Dating Your Josef Originals

Josef Originals are dated with broad strokes. Beginning in 1945 until 1962, they were made in California. The very earliest figures carry a signature in simple block letters, "C" in a circle or "copyright," sometimes a date, and "M. J. George." One Pitty Sing is marked "C 48 M. J. George." When Muriel George examined it, she said, "This is a late one"—1948 to be exact. She had the first one on a shelf in her home. They have been seen signed "Josef" with an "X" marked in the base, as well as "Josef Originals." The figures also had a 5/8" oval sticker, black with a gold border, the lettering "Josef Originals," and under that "California."

Look for Hedy, Teddy, April and Holiday from this period, "Dolls of the Month," little 3-1/4" tall "birthstone" girls, and Oriental figures including Pitty Sing, Cho Cho and Sakura.

Figures were made in Japan from 1959 through the 1980s. The oval sticker kept its size and shape, but instead of "California" they read "Japan," under which they are marked with a 'curl' design, which may be a cursive letter. The ones with a curl also bear a half-inch oval sticker saying "Japan."

This is a most prolific period, without a certain way to date figurines. We have a few clues, however. Mrs. George updated her fashions from time to time. The '60s were the years of very bouffant hairstyles and the beehive. This was followed by long straight hair, which are seldom seen on Josefs. According to Victoria Stocker (Muriel's granddaughter) and George Good, it is difficult to date items made in Japan as the molds were used often. The quality was maintained throughout this period by a triple-firing process, which explains why they do not chip when breakage occurs. A lot of pieces are found with re-glued heads, arms, waists and other places that seem impossible to break without the entire piece shattering—yet it happens.

This book does not deal with pieces made in Taiwan, Korea and Mexico, however, we are told by Victoria Stocker and George Good that figures were made in these countries in the later years, probably as early as the 1970s. We have also been told that Applause is not currently making Josef Originals figurines.

We wish you well in your search for Muriel Joseph George's Josef Originals. She remains an artist worth pursuing.

For More Information

You may contact the authors, Jim and Kaye Whitaker, with any questions. Please send a self-addressed, stamped envelope to P.O. Box 475, Lynnwood, WA 98046.

Anyone interested in joining a collector's club may contact the Josef Collectors Club, c/o Karen Wagner, 13566 Z Street, Omaha, NE, 68137. Again, please send a self-addressed, stamped envelope.

Price Guide

A word about pricing: there are three things that determine pricing: condition, condition and condition! All prices given are for figurines in perfect condition, with no chips, dings, repairs or missing body parts. The current values in this book should be used only as a guide. They are not intended to set prices, which vary greatly from one section of the country to another. Dealer prices normally range from one third to one half of retail. Neither the authors nor the publisher assumes responsibility for any losses that might be incurred as a result of consulting this guide.

page	item	position	price
4	Lambs	TL	$12-14 ea
	Calf	BL	$12-14
	Cow	BL	$16-18
	Shepherds	TR	$24-26 ea
5	Mary & Jesus	TL	$24-26
	Joseph	TL	$22024
	3 Wise men	BR	$24-25 ea
6	Pitty Sing	TL	$45-55
	Pitty Sing	C	$45-55
	Pitty Sing	BL	$45-55
	Yong Chee	R	$55-65
7	Wee Ching	TL	$40-50
	Boy-blue hat	BL	$40-50
	Wee Ching w/dog	C	$40-50
	Girl w/kitten	C	$40-50
	Girl w/kitten	TR	$40-50
	Boy-black hat	BR	$40-50
8	Boy	TL	$40-50
	Boy & Girl with geese	TC	$55-65 ea
	Boy, head/shoulder	TR	$40-50
	Wu Fu	BL	$80-90
	Wu Cha	BR	$80-90
9	Cho Cho	TL	$110-120
	Sakura	CR	$110-120
	Japan	BL	$110-120
	Girl-fan down	BR	$45-55
	Autumn leaf	BR	$45-55
10	Little TV	TL	$75-85
	Girl-Planter	TR	$55-65
	Penny	BL-BC-BR	$55-65 ea
11	The Prince	TC	$55-65
	April/Carol	BL	$50-60 ea
	Teddy/Hedy	BR	$50-60 ea
12	Holiday/Sunny	TC	$50-60 ea
	Boy "Poi"/Girl "Koi"	BL	$50-60 ea
	Bongo/Congo	CR	$50-60 ea
13	Mother w/baby	TL	$85-95
	Mama-Blue, w/book	BL	$85-95
	Mama-Violet	R	$85-95
14	Mary Ann	TL	$35-45
	Mama-Rose	CL	$85-95
	Mary Ann	BL	$35-45
	Mary Ann	TR	$35-45
	Mama-Blue	CR	$85-95
	Mary Ann	BR	$85-95
15	Mama	TL	$85-95
	Mama-Lime Green	BL	$85-95
	Mary Ann	R	$35-45
	Mama	R	$85-95
16	Mary Ann	TL	$35-45
	Mary Ann	TR	$35-45
	Mary Ann	B	$35-45
	Mama	B	$85-95
17	Half Dolls	T	$50-60 ea
	Half Doll	BL	$50-60
	Half Doll	BR	$50-60
18	Molly-Yellow	TL	$50-60
	Sylvia	TC	$50-60
	Molly-Lt. Brown	TR	$50-60
	Victoria	B	$50-60
19	Victoria	TL	$50-60
	Cleo	C	$50-60
	Cleo/Gail	B	$50-60 ea
20	Gail	TL	$50-60
	Charmaine	TC	$60-70
	Cleo	TR	$50-60
	Girl-parasol	BL	$60-70
	Gabrielle/Jacques	BR	$55-65 ea
21	Girl-Blue	TL	$55-65
	Juliette	TC	$55-65
	Charmaine	TR	$55-65
	Girl-Rose	CL	$55-65
	Claudia	BC	$70-80
	Melissa	CR	$70-80
22	Missy	TL	$30-40
	Amy	TR	$70-80
	Joseph II	BL	$55-65
	Kandy/Taffy	BR	$30-40 ea
23	Kandy	TL	$30-40
	Mickey/Melinda	CL	$35-45 ea
	Melinda	BL	$35-45
	Carol	TR	$30-40
	Holly	CR	$30-40
	Cindy	BR	$35-45
24	Denise	TL	$60-70
	Little Gift	CL	$35-45
	Girl/basket	BL	$30-40
	Girl/kitten	C	$30-40
	Party dress	TR	$35-45
	Tea time	CR	$35-45
	Lullaby/Good night	BR	$30-40 ea
25	Girl-lt blue	TL	$30-40
	Little Tutu	CL	$35-45 ea
	Now/Down	BL	$25-35 ea
	Secret Pal rose/green	TR	$30-40 EA
	GL Angel	BR	$40-50
26	Monday	TL	$35-45
	Tuesday	TR	$35-45
	Wednesday	BL	$35-45
	Thursday	BR	$35-45
27	Friday	TL	$35-45
	Saturday	C	$35-45
	Sunday	BR	$35-45
28	Months	All	$25-35 ea
29	Months	All	$25-35 ea
30	Belles	All	$35-45 ea
31	Belles	All	$35-45 ea
32	Months	All	$30-40 ea
33	Months	All	$30-40 ea
34	Atlas	T	$45-55
	Wee three	BL	$40-50
	Kitten	BR	$40-50
35	Countries	All	$30-40 ea
36	Countries	All	$30-40 ea
37	Countries	All	$30-40 ea
38	Countries	All	$30-40 ea
39	Countries	All	$30-40 ea
40	Countries	TL-C-BR	$30-40 ea
	Kabuki	TR	$25-35
	Kabuki	BL	$25-35
41	Tea	TL	$35-45
	Fan	C	$35-45
	Mirror	BR	$35-45
	Housekeepers	TR	$25-35 ea
	Housekeepers	BL	$25-35 ea
42	Cake	TL	$35-45
	w/Butterfly	TC	$35-45
	w/Bird	TR	$35-45
	w/Pekingese	BL	$35-45
	Chinese girl	BC	$35-45
	Moon beam	BR	$30-40
43	Baby/Voyage	T	$30-40
	Birthday	BL	$25-30 ea
	Birthday	BR	$25-35 ea
44	Birthday	TL	$25-35 ea
	Birthday	TR	$25-35 ea
	Birthday	BL-BC-BR	$30-40 ea
45	Birthday	All	$30-40 ea
46	Birthstone	All	$20-25 ea
47	Soap	TL	$20-25
	Pin box	TC	$20-25
	Lipstick	TR	$20-30
	Lipstick	CL	$20-30
	Pray	BL	$20-30
	Rosary	BC	$25-35
	Planter	BR	$30-40
48	Doll of month	All	$25-35 ea
49	Doll of Month	All	$25-35 ea
50	Belles	All	$25-35 ea
51	Belles	All	$25-35 ea
52	Babies	TL	$25-35 ea
	Ballerinas	CL	$25-35 ea
	Ballerinas	BL	$25-35 ea
	Girls	TR	$25-35 ea
	Baby	BR	$30-40
53	Girls	All	$25-35 ea
54	Picture	TL	$25-35
	Pretty	BL	$25-35
	Pisces	TC	$30-40
	Love	TR	$25-35
	Gemini	BC	$30-40
	Violet	BR	$25-35
55	Bride/groom	T	$25-35 ea

Page	Item	Code	Price
	Guest	BL	$25-35
	Bridesmaid	BC	$25-35
	Basket	BR	$25-35
56	New baby	TL	$25-35
	Anniversary	TR	$25-35
	Grad-Pink	BL	$25-35
	Grad girl/boy	BC	$25-35 ea
	Grad-blue	CR	$25-35
57	Jill	TL	$25-35
	Roses	BL	$25-35
	Puppy	TC	$25-35
	Boy/Girl	BC	$25-35
	Present	TR	$25-35
	Poodle	BR	$25-35
58	Girls	All	$25-35 ea
59	Girls	All	$25-35 ea
60	Girls	All	$25-35 ea
61	Girls	All	$25-35 ea
62	Violets	TL	$45-55
	Candle Holder	TR	$25-35
	Book	C	$35-45
	Fan-blue	BL	$45-55
	Fan-peach	BR	$35-45
63	Roses	TL	$35-45
	Brown	TR	$35-45
	Rose	C	$45-55
	Book	BL	$45-55
	Holiday	BR	$55-65
64	Susan	TL	$45-55
	Holiday	TC	$55-65
	Mirror	TR	$35-45
	Summer	BL	$55-65
	Lipstick		$40-50
65	Meg	TL	$45-55
	Corsage	TC	$45-55
	Mary Lou	TR	$45-55
	Pansies	BL	$55-65
	Joy of Spring	BC	$55-65
	Kitten	BR	$65-75
66	Girls	All	$65-75 ea
67	Girls	All	$65-75 ea
68	Girls	All	$100-120 ea
69	Girls	All	$100-120 ea
70	Ladies	All	$110-130 ea
71	Ladies	TL-TC-TR-BC	$100-120 ea
	Ladies	BL-BR	$80-100 ea
72	Colonial	T	$175-185
	Yellow	BL	$80-100
	Marie	BC	$90-110
	Blue	BR	$80-100
73	Ladies	All	$100-120 ea
74	Summer	TL	$75-85
	Winter	TC	$75-85
	Rose garden	C-BR	$60-70 ea
75	Ladies	All	$100-120 ea
76	Ladies	All	$40-50 ea
77	Ladies	All	$65-75 ea
78	Gigi	All	$100-120 ea
79	Ladies	All	$100-120 ea
80	Basket	TL-TR	$80-90 ea
	Nurse	C	$110-130
	Butterfly	BL	$100-120
	Book	BR	$30-40
81	Planter	TL	$100-120
	Writing	TR	$100-120
	Shawl	BL	$90-110
	Reading	BC	$90-110
	Rose	BR	$90-110
82	Ladies	All	$100-120 ea
83	Ladies	All	$100-120 ea
84	Ladies	TL-C-TR	$100-120 ea
	Ladies	BL-BR	$80-100 ea
85	Girls	TL-TC-TR	$75-85 ea
	Girls	BL-BC-BR	$25-30
86	Angel	L	$30-40
	Sweet/baby	R	$30-40 ea
87	Girls	TL-TR-BR	$30-40 ea
	Heart	BL	$75-85
	Theme	C	$80-90
88	Music boxes	All	$80-90 ea
89	Music boxes	All	$80-90 ea
90	Music boxes	All	$80-90 ea
91	Music boxes	TL-TC-TR	$80-90 ea
	Music boxes	BL-BC-BR	$70-80 ea
92	Music boxes	TL-BL	$70-80 ea
	Music box	TR	$80-90
93	Gramaphone	TL	$50-60
	Romance	TR	$60-70
	Swan	C	$70-80
	Bridal	BL	$40-50
	Grace	BR	$40-50
94	Music boxes	TL-BL	$70-80 ea
	Schubert's	TR	$90-100
	Valentine	CR	$25-35
	Hat	BR	$25-35
95	Girls	All	$30-40 ea
96	Angels	All	$25-35 ea
97	Girls	All	$25-35 ea
98	Mugs	TL	$35-45 set
	Puppies	CL	$15-20 ea
	Kids	BL	$25-30 ea
	Snowman	R	$25-35
99	Mary-Jesus	T	$30-40
	Shepherd	T	$25-35
	Reindeer	BL	$25-35 pr
	Deer	BR	$15-20 ea
100	Wee folks	All	$25-30 ea
101	Wee folks	T	$25-35 ea
	Elf	CL	$15-20
	Pixie	CR	$15-20
	Monks	BL	$25-30 ea
	Zodiac	BR	$30-35
102	Girls	All	$20-25 ea
103	January	T	$20-25
	Girls	BL-BC-BR	$25-30 ea
104	Kids	All	$25-35 ea
105	Girls	TL-C-BL	$20-25 ea
	Boy	TR	$25-35
	Flowers	BR	$25-30
106	Girls	TL-TR	$20-25 ea
	Girls	BL-BR	$25-35 ea
107	Large Camel	TR	$50-60
	Small Camel	TR	$25-30
	Mama-Papa Ostrich	BC	$50-60 ea
	Baby Ostriches	BC	$25-30 ea
108	Hippos	TL	$20-25/ $20-25/ $25-30
	Hippo	TR	$20-25
	Kangaroos	C	$15-20/ $35-45
	Elephants	BL	$40-50/ $20-25/ $40-50
	Bull	BR	$18-20
109	Elephant children	TL	$20-25 ea
	Elephant	TR	$20-25
	Elephant kids	BL	$20-25 ea
	Baby	BR	$20-25
	Mama	BR	$40-50
110	Bears	T	$16-18/ $20-25/ $16-18
	Bed bug	CR	$20-25
	Penguin	CL	$20-25
	Horse	B	$40-50
111	Mice	TL	$18-20 ea
	Mice	TR	$16-18 ea
	Soapy/Bride	CL	$18-20 ea
	Grand Dad/kids	BL	$14-16/ $18-20/ $14-16
	Mice	TR	$16-18 ea
	Mice	CR	$16-18 ea
	Mice	BR	$18-20 ea
112	Mice	TL	$16-18/ $18-20
	Mice	CL	$16-18 ea
	Papa	BL	$18-20
	Kids	BL	$16-18
	Nurse	BL	$18-20
	Mice	TR	$18-20 ea
	Mice	CR	$16-18 ea
	Grad	BR	$18-20
	Bow	BR	$16-18
	Candle	BR	$18-20
113	Planter	TL	$40-50
	Mice	CL	$16-18/ $18-20/ $16-18
	Mice	BL	$18-20 ea
	Mice	TR	$18-20/ $16-18/ $18-20
	Mice	CR	$18-20 ea
	Mice	BR	$16-20 ea
114	Mother w/litter	TL	$15-20 set
	Mom w/kittens	CL	$18-20 ea
	Kittens	BL	$18-22 ea
	Mom/kittens	CR	$18-22 ea
	Cat	BR	$18-22
115	Christmas	TL	$18-22 ea
	Siamese	CL	$18-22 ea
	Cats	BL	$18-22 ea
	Kitten/Mom	TR	$18-22 ea
	Dad/Mom w/kitten	CR	$18-22/ $18-25
	Dad-Mom-Kittens	BR	$18-22 ea
116	6 kittens	TC	$18-22 ea
	3 kittens	C	$18-22 ea
	Kittens	CL	$18-22 ea
	Kittens w/turtle	CR	$18-22 ea
	5 kittens	BL	$18-22 ea
	2 cats	BR	$18-22 ea
117	Music boxes	TC	$25-35 ea
	Music box	CL	$25-35
	4 puppies	BL	$18-22 ea
	2 puppies	CR	$18-22 ea
	2 boxers	BR	$18-22 ea
118	Fox	TL	$18-22
	Chihuahua	CL	$18-22
	Monkeys	BL	$16-18 ea
	2 Dogs	TR	$18-22 ea
	Dog	CR	$22-26
	Monkeys	BR	$16-18 ea
119	Group	T	$16-18 ea
	Bees	CL	$18-22 ea
	Caterpillers	BL	$12-14 ea
	Turtle/bug	R	$12-14 ea
120	Frogs	T	$14-16 ea
	Frog	C	$14-16
	Rooster	C	$14-16
	Turtle	C	$14-16
	Frogs	BL	$16-18 ea
	Frogs	BR	$16-18 ea
121	Rabbits	TL	$24-26 ea
	Skunk	CL	$18-22
	Mama/baby	BL	$24-26 ea
	Rabbits	TR	$18-22/ $24-26
	Bunny	CR	$16-18
	Rabbits	BR	$16-18 ea
122	Ducks w/ caterpiller	T	$35-45 set
	Pigs	CL-CR	$14-18 ea
	Duck family	BL	$35-45 set
	Mama/baby	BR	$18-20/ $12-14
123	Music box	TC	$25-35
	Pig	BL	$16-18
	Owls	C	$12-14 ea
	Pie bird	R	$25-30

Index